Who Killed My Father

ÉDOUARD LOUIS

Who Killed My Father

*translated from the French
by Lorin Stein*

A NEW DIRECTIONS BOOK

Originally published as *Qui a tué mon père* by Éditions Le Seuil

First published as a New Directions Book in 2019
Manufactured in the United States of America
New Directions Books are printed on acid-free paper
Design by Erik Rieselbach

Library of Congress Cataloging-in-Publication Data
Names: Louis, Édouard, author. | Stein, Lorin, translator.
Title: Who killed my father? / Édouard Louis ; translated
by Lorin Stein.
Other titles: Qui a tué mon pere. English
Description: New York : New Directions, 2019.
Identifiers: LCCN 2018046580 | ISBN 9780811228503 (alk. paper)
Subjects: LCSH: Louis, Édouard—Family. | Authors, French—
20th century—Biography. | Authors, French—21st century—
Biography. | Fathers of authors—France—Biography. |
Louis family.
Classification: LCC PQ2712.O895 Z4613 2019 | DDC 843/.92 [B] —dc23
LC record available at https://lccn.loc.gov/2018046580

10 9 8 7 6 5 4 3 2 1

New Directions Books are published for James Laughlin
by New Directions Publishing Corporation
80 Eighth Avenue, New York 10011

for Xavier Dolan

Acknowledgments

This book in its current form would have been impossible without the writings of Claudia Rankine, Ocean Vuong, Tash Aw, and Peter Handke, especially Handke's *A Sorrow Beyond Dreams* and Aw's *The Face*. It would also have been impossible without the films of Terrence Malick: I don't know how often I rewatched *To the Wonder* and *The Tree of Life* while the book was being revised (several dozen times at least). Nor would this text have come into being without Litteraturhuset in Oslo, Yale University, the New School, and MIT, where I presented early versions of certain chapters, not to mention the periodicals *Morgenbladet* in Norway, *Dagens Nyheter* in Sweden, *FAS* in Germany, and *Freeman's* in the United States, where those versions were published. I must also thank Stanislas Nordey, who was present at the origin of this text, who supported it with his solar energy, and who was its first reader. And, of course, this book could never have existed without Didier or Geoffroy.

Who Killed My Father

IF THIS WERE *a text for the theater, here is how it would begin: A father and son stand a few feet apart in a vast empty space. That space could be a wheat field, an abandoned factory, the laminated floor of a school gym. Maybe it's snowing. Maybe the snow slowly buries them, until they disappear. The father and son almost never look at each other. The son is the only one to speak. At first he reads aloud, from a sheet of paper or a screen. He addresses his father, but his father doesn't seem to hear, we don't know why not.*

11

Although they stand close together, neither can reach the other. Sometimes they touch, they come into physical contact, but even in these moments they are apart. The son speaks, and only the son, and this does violence to them both: the father is never allowed to tell his own story, while the son longs for a response that he will never receive.

I.

WHEN ASKED WHAT *the word* racism *means to her, the American scholar Ruth Gilmore has said that racism is the exposure of certain populations to premature death.*

The same definition holds with regard to male privilege, to hatred of homosexuality or trans people, to domination by class—to social and political oppression of all kinds. If we look at politics as the government of some living people by other living people, as well as the existence of individuals within communities not of their

13

choosing, then politics is what separates some populations, whose lives are supported, nurtured, protected, from other populations, who are exposed to death, to persecution, to murder.

Last month I came to see you in the small northern town where you've been living. It's a gray, ugly town. The sea is just a few miles away, but you never go. I hadn't seen you for months—it had been a long time. At first when you opened the door, I didn't recognize you.

I looked at you. In your face I read the signs of the years I'd been away.

Later, the woman you live with explained that by now you can hardly walk. She also told me that when you sleep you need a breathing machine or else your heart will stop. It can't beat without assistance, without the help of a machine. It doesn't want to. When you got up to go to the bathroom, just walking the thirty feet there and back left you winded. I saw for myself, you had to sit and catch your breath. You apologized. These apologies are a new thing with you, I have to get used to them. You told me that you suffer from an acute form of diabetes and from high cholesterol, that you could have a heart attack at any moment. As you were telling me all this, you ran out of breath. Your chest emptied of air as though it had sprung a leak. Even talking required too intense, too great an effort. I saw you struggling with your body, but I pretended not to. The week before, you'd had an operation for what the doctors call a ventral hernia—I'd never heard of it. Your body has grown too heavy for itself. Your belly stretches toward the floor. It is overstretched, so badly overstretched that it has ruptured your abdominal lining. Your belly has been torn apart by its own weight, its own mass.

You can't drive anymore. You're not allowed to drink. You can't take a shower or go to work, except at great risk. You're barely fifty years old. You belong to the category of humans whom politics has doomed to an early death.

I spent my childhood longing for your absence. I would return from school late in the afternoon, around five o'clock. I knew that if I reached our house and your car wasn't parked out front, it meant that you were at the café or at your brother's and that you'd come home late, maybe after dark. If I didn't see your car out front I knew we'd eat without you. Sooner or later my mother would shrug and give us our dinner, and I wouldn't see you till morning. Every day, when I reached our street, I thought of your car and prayed: let it not be there, let it not be there, let it not be there.

It's only by accident that I've come to know you. Or through other people. Not long ago

I asked my mother how you met, and why she fell in love with you. *The cologne*, she said. *He wore cologne and you know in those days it wasn't like now. Men didn't wear cologne. But your father did. He was different. He smelled so good.*

He was the one who pursued me, she went on. *I'd just split up with my first husband, I'd finally got him out of my life, and I was happier that way, without a man. Women always are. But your father kept at it. He was always showing up with chocolate or flowers. So in the end I gave in. I just gave in.*

2002 That day my mother caught me dancing, all by myself, in my room. I'd been trying to move as quietly as possible. I'd tried not to make any noise, not to breathe too hard. The music wasn't turned up, either, but she heard something through the wall and came in to

see what was going on. I was startled and out
of breath, my heart in my throat, my lungs in
my throat. I turned to face her and waited—
my heart in my throat, my lungs in my throat.
I expected her to scold me, or mock me, but
she said, with a smile, that when I danced was
when I looked the most like you. *Dad used to
dance?* I asked. Hearing that your body had
done something so free, so beautiful, and so at
odds with your obsession with masculinity, it
dawned on me that you might once have been
a different person. My mother nodded. *Your father was always dancing! Everywhere he went.
And when he danced, everybody watched. I was so
proud to have a man like that!* I ran through the
house and into the courtyard where you were
chopping wood for winter. I wanted to know
whether it was true. I wanted proof. I told you
what she'd just told me and you looked away.
*You can't go believing all the crap your mother tells
you,* you said in a halting voice. But you were
blushing. You were lying, I could tell.

*

One evening I was home alone because you
and the others were out having dinner with
friends and I hadn't wanted to go. I remember the wood stove spreading its scent of ash
through the house and its warm orange glow.
In an old family album, worm-eaten and mil-
dewed, I found some photos of you dressed as
a woman, as a cheerleader. All my life I'd seen
you sneer at any sign of femininity in a man.
I'd heard you say a man should never *act like a
girl*, ever. You must have been thirty in those
pictures, I must already have been born. I
pored over those images all night long—your
body, your body in a skirt, the wig on your
head, the lipstick on your mouth, the fake
breasts under your tee shirt. You must have
stuffed cotton wadding in a bra. The most
surprising thing to me was that you looked
happy. You were smiling. I stole one of the

photos and several times a week I would take it out of the drawer where I'd hidden it and try to decipher it. I never mentioned it to you.

One day I wrote in a notebook, thinking of you: *To write the story of his life would mean writing the story of my absence.*

Another time, I surprised you while you were watching an opera telecast on TV. You'd never done that before, not in front of me. When the soprano sang her lament I saw that your eyes were glistening.

What is most incomprehensible is that even those who cannot always bring themselves to respect the norms and rules imposed by the world still insist that they be respected, like you when you said a man should never cry.

Did it make you suffer, that paradox? Were

you ashamed of crying, you who were always saying a man should never cry?

I wanted to say *I cry, too. Plenty. All the time.*

2001 Another winter evening. You'd invited people over to eat with us—a large group of friends. This wasn't something you often did, and I had the idea of putting on a show for you and the other grown-ups. I invited all the children at the table—there were three boys besides me—to come to my room so we could prepare and rehearse. I had decided that we would put on a little performance imitating a pop group called Aqua (long since forgotten). I worked on the choreography for more than an hour, the steps, the gestures. I told everyone what to do. I would be the lead singer—her name was Lene. The other boys would be the backup singers and musicians, strumming invisible guitars. I led the way into the dining room. The others followed. I gave the signal and we started the show, but as soon as we did, you turned away. I couldn't understand it. All the grown-ups were watching except for you. I sang louder. I danced harder to make you notice me, but you weren't watching. I said, *Look, Dad, look.* I was putting up a fight, but you weren't looking.

When you drove I used to demand, *Do Formula 1!* And you'd hit the gas, you'd go a hundred miles an hour on those little country roads. It scared my mother. She'd scream, she'd call you a lunatic—and you would catch my eye in the rearview mirror and smile.

You were born into a family of six or seven children. Your father worked in a factory. Your mother didn't work. Poverty was all they knew. I have almost nothing more to say about your early childhood.

Your father left when you were five years

old. This is a story I often tell. One morning he went off to work at the factory and that night he didn't come home. Your mother, my grandmother, told me that she waited for him. That's all she'd ever done anyway. That's how she'd spent the first part of her life, waiting for him. *I'd made him something to eat, we waited for him as usual, but he never came back.* Your father drank a lot, and certain nights, because of the drinking, he used to hit your mother. He would snatch up plates, small objects, sometimes even chairs, and throw them right at her. Then he'd come at her with his fists. I don't know whether your mother cried out or endured the pain in silence. As for you, you watched without being able to do anything, powerless, trapped in the body of a child.

That, too, is something I've already told— but shouldn't I repeat myself when talking about your life, since nobody wants to hear stories about lives like yours? Should I not repeat myself until they listen to us? To *make* them listen to us? Should I not cry out?

I am not afraid of repeating myself because what I am writing, what I am saying, does not answer to the standards of literature, but to those of necessity and desperation, to standards of fire.

I've already said: When your father died, you celebrated the news. You had never forgotten what he'd done to your mother. Your sister had tried to make peace between you several times. She had come and asked you to forget the past. She herself had forgiven him. But whenever she came to visit, you'd concentrate on whatever TV show you were watching and act as if you didn't know she was there. The day you learned that your father was dead, the whole family happened to be in the kitchen. It was the same day or the same week as your fortieth birthday. Once again we were watching TV, and you said loud enough for everyone to hear, *This calls for a toast.* Looking back, I think you said it too loud, there was something off about your tone, something artificial, as if it were a line you'd been working on for months. You took the car to go buy a bottle of pastis at the village grocery. You partied all night, you laughed, you sang.

It's strange: because your father was violent toward you, you were always saying—obsessively—that you would never be violent with us, that you'd never hit a child of your own. *I will never raise a hand against one of my kids, so long as I live.* Violence doesn't just lead to violence. It was a phrase I repeated for years, that violence causes violence, but I was mistaken. Violence had saved us from violence.

Your father wasn't the only one to have a problem with alcohol. Alcohol was part of your life from before you were born. We used to hear one story after another: the car accidents, a fatal fall on a patch of ice after a hard-drinking dinner, conjugal violence fueled by wine and pastis. Drinking brought oblivion. The world was responsible, but how could you blame the world, the world that imposed a life that the people around us had no choice but to try to forget—with drinking, by drinking.

It was forget or die, or forget and die.

Forget or die, or forget and die of the rage to forget.

The night I put on a show for you with the other children, I was determined, I didn't want to stop. I wanted you to look at me. Embarrassment began to spread through the room, and still I went on begging, *Look, Dad, look.*

1998 It's Christmas. I reconstruct the image as best I can, but reality has the quality of dreams: the harder I try to grasp it, the more it slips away. The whole family is sitting around the table. I am eating far too much: you brought home too much food for our Christmas dinner. You were always afraid of being different because of lack of money. You'd say: *I don't see why we should be any different from anyone else.* And for that reason you wanted our table to have everything you imagined other people having and eating for Christmas—foie gras, oysters, bûches de Noël—so that, paradoxically, the poorer we were, the more money we spent for fear of not being like other people.

I'm talking to my mother and brothers and sisters, but not to you. You won't talk. You say you hate the holidays. When December comes, you say you wish the holidays were already over and done with and well behind us, and I think you pretend to hate happiness in order to make yourself believe that, if your life seems an unhappy one, at least you're the one who chose it. As if you wanted to pretend you had some control over your own unhappiness. As if you wanted to give the impression that, if your life was too hard, you wanted it that way, out of disgust with pleasure, out of a loathing for joy.

I think you refuse to acknowledge defeat.

At Christmas, every year, you would hide the presents in the trunk of the car. You'd wait until I'd gone off to bed, then you'd bring them in and put them under the tree for me to find when I woke up the next day.

But that night—it was almost midnight, we weren't asleep—I heard, we all heard, an explosion outside. It was as if the kitchen had exploded, that's how intense it was, how immense—I don't know how to describe it—as if an airplane had come crashing down on our doorstep or in the backyard. I can't find an image to express it. You went outside to see what was going on. I followed you, and I saw: your car was there, but compressed, reduced to a shapeless lump of metal. All around it were scattered little shards of plastic, with scraps of shredded wrapping paper floating in the air. And then, finally, a few feet past the vanished car, there was an enormous tractor trailer, a car-hauler, with a slight scrape on its bumper.

The man driving it—the man responsible for all this—had paused to contemplate the tragedy. From where I stood, I could see the condensation rising from his mouth, the plumes of smoke blurring his face. He looked like a ghost. When he saw us, he threw his truck into reverse and vanished into the night. You chased him, which made no sense. You could never have caught up with a truck. It was hopeless, completely hopeless, but you ran shouting, *I'm going to kill you, you motherfucking son of a bitch*. I watched you run after him. Your body disappeared into the darkness, dissolved in the shadows, then reappeared, defeated and out of breath.

I was too young to remember, but I remember, the look on your face as you gazed down at the remains of the car. Seeing the look on your face made me cry, and I asked what you'd do now about getting to the factory. I lay down on the sofa and cried all Christmas Eve. Why did I cry? I should have been crying because my presents had disappeared. (I'd figured it out. I knew you hid them in the car.) At the age of seven, I shouldn't have been crying over the car. I ought to have been thinking about my presents—that would have been the logical thing. Had you already taught me that we were the sort of people whom nobody would come to help? Had you already conveyed to me your sense of our place in the world?

It often seems to me that I love you.

When I asked about you, my mother told me that your father's disappearance left the family even more destitute than before. Your mother found herself alone with six or seven children. She'd never finished school. She couldn't find work. Peter Handke says: "For a woman to be born under such conditions was itself deadly." And yet my mother also said you were much happier, because the man of the family had disappeared, along with his violence, and your fear of his reactions, of his masculine insanity.

What we call history is nothing but the story of the same emotions, the same joys, reproduced across bodies and time, and my mother experienced that same feeling of happiness when she threw you out of the house. One of those weeknights when you didn't come home because you were at your brother's or at the café, when you kept my mother waiting, she stuffed your clothes into garbage bags and threw them out the window, onto the sidewalk. I was grown up, I was eighteen, I was no longer living at home, but she told me what happened. You had gone off with your buddies and hadn't told her when you'd be back. For years she, too, had done nothing but wait for you, the way your mother had waited for your father, but that night she'd had enough.

You had lived together twenty-five years. You came home in the middle of the night but the door was locked. You pounded the walls, the windows. You shouted. You didn't yet understand what your clothes were doing on the sidewalk, or you pretended not to understand. Through the door my mother shouted at you never to come back. *Never?* you asked. She repeated her words: *Never ever.* It was over. Once you were gone she was never, as she said herself, the same person. Not yet fifty, she went off to live in a big city for the first time in her life. She traveled. She discovered new passions and, especially, new objects of scorn. She took to saying, "Ugh, these hicks!" as if she hadn't lived in the country all her life.

The night of the pretend concert, even though I was running out of breath, I didn't want to let it go. I don't know how long I kept it up, how long I went on insisting, *Look, Dad, look.*

Finally you stood up and said, *I'm going outside for a smoke.* I had hurt your feelings.

You never got over the separation from my mother. It destroyed something inside you. As always happens, being apart made you realize how much you loved her. After the breakup, you became more sensitive to the world. You got sick more often. Everything hurt. It is as if the pain of the separation had opened up a wound and everything around you—your world in all its violence—came rushing in

When you were in a good mood, you used to call my mother "Choupette," "Bibiche," "Maman."

You'd swat her on the ass in front of other people and she'd say, *Cut it out, don't you have any class?* You'd laugh. And that would make her laugh.

She used to complain that you never gave her anything but vacuum cleaners, pans, or housewares for her birthday: *After all, it's not like I'm some kind of maid.*

She told me, *Every time we have a fight, your father swears he'll change. He'll never change. It's like they say, a dog that's bit before will bite again.*

The night of the pretend concert, did I hurt your feelings because I chose to play the singer—the girl?

You didn't study. For you, dropping out of school as fast as possible was a matter of masculine pride. It was the rule in the world you lived in: *be a man, don't act like a girl, don't be a faggot.* Only girls and those others—the ones suspected of being deviant, of being abnormal—would submit to school rules, to punishments, to what the teachers asked or demanded.

For you, constructing a masculine body

meant resisting the school system. It meant
not submitting to orders, to Order. It even
meant standing up to school and the au-
thority it embodied. In grade school one of
my cousins slapped a teacher in front of the
whole class. We always spoke of him as a hero.
Masculinity—*don't act like a girl, don't be a faggot*—meant that you dropped out as fast as
you could to show everyone you were strong,
as soon as you could to show you were rebel-
lious, and so, as far as I can tell, constructing
your masculinity meant depriving yourself
of any other life, any other future, any other
prospect that school might have opened up.
Your manhood condemned you to poverty,
to lack of money. Hatred of homosexuality =
poverty.

There's something I'd like to try to put into
words: When I think about it now, I feel as
though your existence was, against your will—
indeed, against your very being—a negative

existence. You *didn't* have money, you *couldn't* finish school, you *couldn't* travel, you *couldn't* realize your dreams. It is hard to describe your life in anything but negative terms.

In his book *Being and Nothingness*, Jean-Paul Sartre probes the connection between one's being and one's actions. Are we defined by what we do? Are we defined by the projects we undertake? Are a woman and a man simply what they do, or is there a difference, a gap, between the truth of who we are and our actions?

Your life proves that we are not what we do, but rather that *we are what we haven't done*, because the world, or society, stood in our way. Because *verdicts*, as Didier Eribon calls them, came crashing down on us—gay, trans, female, black, poor—and made certain lives, certain experiences, certain dreams, inaccessible to us.

2004 In grade school, for the first time, I hear about the Cold War, about how Germany was divided in two, how Berlin had been separated by a wall, and how the wall came down. The fact that a major city, not so far away from us, could be divided in two, practically overnight, by a wall, came over me like a storm. I was fascinated. For the rest of the day I couldn't pay attention to anything that anyone was saying. It was all I could think of. I was trying to imagine this wall set down in the middle of a street that, just the day before, women and men could cross without a second thought.

You were already more than twenty years old when the wall was destroyed, so the entire rest of the day I fantasized about the questions I would ask you: Did you know people who'd seen the wall? Did you know women or men who'd actually touched it, who had participated in its destruction? Tell me, what exactly was this Europe divided in two, this cement wall between one Europe and another?

The bus that took me home dropped me at the village square, but for once I didn't dawdle as long as possible or loiter in the street.

I didn't pray that your car wouldn't be out front. I ran—I'd never run so fast—my head filled with all my questions.

I asked you all the questions that had piled up in my head. *Yeah, yeah,* you answered vaguely. *It's true, there was a wall. They talked about it on TV.* That was all you said. I waited for more, but you turned away. I insisted. *But tell me, what was it like? What exactly was it? What did the wall look like? If you loved someone who lived on the other side of the wall, could you never see them again, ever?* You had nothing to say. I started to see that my nagging was causing you pain. I was twelve, but I used words you didn't understand. All the same, I pushed a tiny bit more and you lost your temper. You snapped at me, told me to stop asking questions. But it wasn't the way you usually lost your temper. It wasn't normal, the way you snapped. You were ashamed because I was confronting you with a school culture that had excluded you, that had wanted you out. Where is history? The his-

tory they taught at school was not your own.
We were learning world history, and you
were left out.

1999 I'm counting on my fingers: one, two,
three, four, five, six, seven, eight. Soon I'll be
eight years old. You asked me what I wanted
for my birthday and I told you: *Titanic*. The
videocassette had just come out. We kept
seeing the ad on TV. They played it over and
over, several times a day. I don't know why
I was so drawn to the movie. I couldn't say.
Was it the love story? Was it Leonardo Di-
Caprio and Kate Winslet's shared dream of
becoming a different person? Was it Kate
Winslet's beauty? I don't know. But I was
already obsessed with this movie I hadn't
yet seen, and it's what I asked for. You answered that it was a movie for girls and that
I shouldn't want something like that. But I'm
going too fast—first you begged me to want
something else: *Wouldn't you prefer a remote*

control car or a superhero outfit? Think hard now. But I said, *No, no,* Titanic's *what I want,* and it was only after I insisted, only after you failed, that your tone changed. In that case, you told me, I wouldn't get anything, no present at all. I don't remember whether I cried. The days passed. The morning of my birthday I found, there at the foot of my bed, a large white box and on it, written in golden letters, *Titanic.* Inside was the cassette, but also a coffee-table book about the movie, maybe also a model of the ship. It was a collector's edition, certainly more than you could afford, more than we could afford, but you'd bought it and put it beside my bed, all wrapped up. I kissed you on the cheek and you didn't say anything. You let me watch that movie almost a dozen times a week for more than a year.

The night of the pretend concert, did I hurt your feelings because I played the part of a girl and because you thought your friends would judge you for it—because they'd hold you responsible for having brought me up like a girl?

You were afraid of rats and bats. I don't know why those animals in particular.

You'd eat fistfuls of grated cheese, your mouth over the wide-open bag. I'd see the bits of cheese falling back into the bag—falling from your mouth back into the bag—and I'd complain: *I don't want to eat cheese that's been in your mouth!*

You dreamed of working in a morgue. You used to say, *At least the dead don't bust your balls.*

After the pretend concert, I found you outside chain smoking. You were alone, in a tee shirt. It was cold, the street was empty, and I felt the almost infinite noiselessness, the silence, filling my mouth and my ears. You looked at the ground. I told you, *I'm sorry, Dad*. You took me in your arms and said, *It's nothing. Forget it, it's nothing.*

*

For five years you tried to be young. When you left high school—just a few days after you started—you were hired at the village factory, but you didn't stay there long, either, barely a couple of weeks. You didn't want to repeat the life of your father and his father before him. They'd gone straight to work the moment childhood was over, at fourteen or fifteen. They had gone, without any transition, from childhood to exhaustion and getting ready to die, without ever having been granted those few years of oblivion toward the world and reality that others call youth (even if that's a silly way of putting it, *those few years of oblivion others call youth*).

But for five years you fought for youth with

all your might. You went to live in the south of France, telling yourself that life would be better there, less oppressive, if only because of all the sunshine. You stole mopeds, you stayed out all night, you drank all you could. You lived as intensely and aggressively as possible, because you felt that these experiences were stolen—and this, this is my point: there are those to whom youth is given and those who can only try desperately to steal it.

Then one day you stopped. I think it was a question of money, but not only that. You stopped everything you were doing and went back to the village where you were born—or the one right next to it—and you got yourself hired by the factory where your whole family had worked before you.

A classic pattern: because you felt that you hadn't lived your youth to the fullest, you spent your whole life trying to be young. That's the trouble with stolen things, like you with your youth: we can never quite believe they are really ours, and so we have to keep stealing them forever. The theft never ends. You wanted to recapture your youth, to reclaim it, to resteal it. Only those who have always had everything given to them can truly feel what it is to possess. A sense of possession is not something one can acquire.

One of those attempts to be young again— to be young at last—took place when you were with your friend Anthony. Do you remember? The two of you were in the car and you spotted the police behind you. You'd both had a lot to drink. They would have taken your license away if they'd stopped you, and would never have given it back. You thought they were tailing you, so you hit the gas. You took off, as if they were in hot pursuit. You ran lights, you went faster and faster. I imagine you were acting out the chase scenes you watched all night on TV, with American cops and robbers: even in the most intense moments of our lives, it seems to me, we continue to act out scenes and roles we've seen in books or movies. You drove till you came to a river.

You both leapt out of the car and into the water to keep from getting caught by the police (I'm not sure if the police were ever actually chasing you in the first place). You swam—you, who were more frightened of water than anything, who were afraid of taking a bath, that's how bad your phobia was, you swam in the freezing water, and together you climbed out a few hundred feet downstream. For a long time you waited there, up to your ankles in mud, soaked to the skin, hoping the police would go away, and then you came home to my mother's, your clothes soggy with water smelling of muck and of fish. The water was pouring off you, off your bodies onto the floor, the drops streaming down the fabric of your clothing and puddling in silence at your feet. You didn't use to tell this story yourself, since you never talked much, but when my mother told it—as she often did, two or three times a month—you would smile and say, *It's true we had a good laugh.* You had managed to retrieve a moment of your youth.

You were fascinated by all technological innovations, as if, through the novelty they embodied, you could infuse your own life with a newness to which you were not entitled. You commented, in a voice part envy and part admiration, on ads for new phones, tablets, or computers. You didn't buy them, they cost too much. You made do with gadgets traveling salesmen hawked at the village market: a watch that went backwards, a machine for making Coke at home, a laser that could project the image of a naked woman on a wall a hundred yards away. *In general, these memories are inhabited more by things than by people.*

You lived out your youth through the youth of these things.

And another thing: every September the village set up amusement rides for the harvest fair, with shooting galleries and slot machines. You'd spend our monthly budget in four days—the money that was meant to cover our food, our bills, our rent. My mother used to say, *I didn't marry a man, I married a kid.*

(I speak of you in the past tense because I don't know you anymore. The present tense would be a lie.)

An image: It's summer. It's nighttime in the middle of the day. Darkness covers the immensity of the earth. It covers us, you and me and the cornfield where I stand beside you. It may be noon but it's dark out. You tell me, *Solar eclipse.* You tell me, *Don't take off your glasses or the moon will burn your eyes and you'll never see anything again.* You tell me, *This is a one-time thing. The next time something like this happens on Earth we'll all be dead. All of us. Even you.*

(you'd given me that watch that went back-
ward, the one you bought at the market. I lost
it.)

Another image: You're driving. I'm sitting in
the seat behind you. It's just us, and you say,
We're going to drive on the waves. I don't know
what that means. I've never heard this expression before. You say it again, *We're going to
drive on the waves*, and you take off straight
for the sea. You drive us onto the sand and
the sea comes closer and closer. The waves are
coming toward us. I think you want to kill us.
I think you want to die and that you want to
take me with you. I scream *No Dad, no, please!* I
close my eyes, I don't want to die. You get even
closer, and then, just at the water's edge, you
give the steering wheel a neat, quick turn—
and now you're driving us, no longer into the
waves, but alongside them, two wheels on
sand and two in the water, with part of the
car submerged by a foot or a foot-and-a-half.

I slide over in my seat. I look out the window
and it's true: all I can see is water and your car
driving over it, over the surface of the water.
Nothing else. *See? Just like I said. We are driving on the waves.*

I've forgotten almost everything I told you
when I came to see you for the last time, but
I remember all the things I didn't tell you. In
general, when I look back on the past and our
life together, what I remember most is what
I didn't tell you. My memories are of what
didn't take place.

And after all those years of fighting for your
right to be young—you got married. Everything happened in sequence.

When my mother met you she already had
two children by her first husband, the one
who preceded you. Right away you wanted
to treat them as your own. You slept beside

them when they were afraid at night, even though they were already big kids. You suggested they take your last name. Was this a desire to pass for a good father in the eyes of others, or was it pure love? The line between these two things is always too fine for anyone to call. You slapped me the time I said my big brother was only my half brother. *He's your brother*, you said. *There are no half brothers in this house, none of my kids is a half.*

2006 I've nearly finished: I have hardly anything left to tell. This is one of the last scenes—after this it's all blank. The scene takes place on a bus, on the seat of a school bus upholstered in a kind of grimy blue-and-green carpeting. There I sit. Down the aisle, three or four rows ahead of me, is my cousin Jayson. He's laughing. But he's not laughing in a normal way. He sings. He shouts. The driver tells him to knock it off. Jayson won't. He doesn't understand what's being said to him, he's having one of his seizures. He was born with a handicap that makes him have seizures several times a month, though it's impossible to predict when they'll come, and he can't stop, he can't hear what's going on around him. The driver tells him a second time to knock it off, and Jayson laughs even harder, in a more and more unruly way, so the driver stops the bus with a jerk. He pulls the hand brake, gets out of his seat, and comes toward my cousin to hit him. He had already grabbed Jayson by the back of his tee shirt when I understood what was going on, what was about to happen. He had lifted his other hand to hit him across the face, but just then I stood up (I don't know what happened, it wasn't like me, I wasn't a brave person) and told him he shouldn't pick on a kid with a handicap. His hand stops in midair, he spins around, and comes toward me. I don't move. And I'm the one he slaps.

When I came home that night I told you.

You listened, already stiffening, breathing hard, and you told me you'd take revenge. I asked you not to. I was afraid of the consequences of your revenge (I know how these things go), but it was too late. The next day you waited in the village square. You got on the bus when it stopped, you grabbed the driver by the throat and told him never to touch me again. The other children seemed to admire you. They even smiled at me: your strength reflected on me. But the next day, the kids who had seen you threaten the driver told me I didn't know how to defend myself, that I needed my father to defend me. For several months they teased me and before I could say anything back, before I could react, they'd say: *What are you going to do, call your father?*

(though I almost never called you)

On the train to that town where you live now, I wrote the other day: *Other people, society, the law never stop avenging us, unaware that their vengeance, far from helping us, destroys us. They mean to save us by their vengeance, but they destroy us.*

II.

I WASN'T INNOCENT. In 2001 my big brother tried to kill him—tried to kill my father. It was a few days after the World Trade Center attacks, and that's why I remember the date it happened. Or rather, why I can't forget. My big brother and I had watched the twin towers catch fire, implode, then collapse. My brother drank a whole bottle of whiskey in front of the TV, trying to drown his grief, and he wept and wept. I remember him saying *Now the bastards are going to kill us all.* That's what he said. *They're going to kill us all. They*

just started a war, I'm telling you. Get ready,
because I'm telling you, we're all going to die.
The next bomb they drop, it's going to be on us.
On the French. And then, I'm telling you, we're
fucked. For a long time I thought it was my
father who had said these things, but now I remember it wasn't him, it was my brother. I was
nine years old, and I was crying, too, the way
a child does when he sees his family cry, without really understanding, precisely because of
my own inability to understand, because of
this void, crying because I was afraid of death
and because I was too young to realize that
my brother's words were only the expression
of his own violent and paranoid impulses.
They were the words of a man I would come
to hate two or three years later.

A week later, with no connection to the attacks apart from the proximity of the dates,
which lets me place the murder attempt in

time, my big brother, right in the middle of dinner, grabbed my father by the throat in front of our whole family and started slamming his back against the kitchen wall. He was killing him. It wasn't the first time those two had fought. My father was yelling, and begging him—I'd never seen my father beg before—and my big brother was screaming, *You son of a bitch I'll fucking murder you*, the same words, the same phrases over and over again. Meanwhile my mother and Deborah, a girl whom my brother had just met, tried to shield me. I can still see my mother. She was throwing glasses at my big brother to make him stop, but each time she missed, and the glasses shattered on the floor. She was yelling, too, *Don't do it, you two, please for fuck's sake, calm down*. She was—I don't know how to put it, she was braying, she was bellowing, *He's going to kill his father, he's going to kill his own father*, then she whispered to me, *Don't look, baby, don't look. Mommy's here. Don't look.*

But I wanted to look. Because I was the one who had started the fight between my brother and my father. I'd done it on purpose. It was my revenge.

The story of my revenge begins very early one morning. You have to imagine the scene: I'm having my hot chocolate in the kitchen, sitting next to my mother and big brother. They've just woken up, and they're smoking and watching TV. They've only been awake for twenty minutes, but already they've smoked three or four cigarettes apiece, and the air feels saturated with their thick cloudy smoke. I cough. My mother and brother laugh at the TV, wheezily, and smoke some more. My father and my sisters aren't there.

I tell my mother that I have to go see a friend in the village, I'm supposed to help fix his bike. She nods without looking away from the TV. Silently I get dressed. I leave the house. I hear her laugh again. I close the door behind me and venture out into the cold, into that world of red and gray brick and the smell of dung and fog, and then I realize that I've left something, I don't remember what, in my bedroom, so I turn around.

When I enter the house, without knocking, I see, next to the crackling stove, the silhouettes of my mother and brother enveloped in smoke. They're sitting closer together than before. What's more, I can tell what's going on: my mother is giving my big brother money. She's taking advantage of the dim light, and the fact that the others are away, to give him some money. And I know my father has forbidden my mother to do this. He has ordered her never to give my brother any more money, ever, because he knows that if my brother has money he'll buy alcohol and drugs and, once he's drunk and stoned, he'll go out and tag supermarkets and bus stops or set fire to the bleachers in the village stadium.

He's done it several times before. They could have put him in jail. My father told my mother, *Don't let me catch you giving that delinquent any money.* So when my mother sees me standing there, she gave a start. She comes up to me, in a rage, and says, *You better not tell your father or you'll be sorry,* then she hesitates. She hesitates over which strategy to adopt. She tries another tack, and changing her tone, she starts over in a gentler, more imploring voice. *Your brother needs money for his school lunch, but your father can't get that through his head. Be nice to Mommy and don't tell Dad. You know how he can get.* So I agree not to say anything. I promise I won't say a word.

My mother makes a fatal blunder fifteen days later. She has no way of knowing that, by the end of the day, she will pay. That she'll suffer. That morning I'm alone with her. Neither of us is speaking. I'm getting ready for school, and when I open the door to leave she says to me, for no apparent reason, between two drags on her cigarette, something she'd often said to me before but never so harshly and never so directly, until then: *Why are you like that? Why do you always go around acting like a girl? Everyone in the village says you're a faggot, it's a goddamn disgrace. They all make fun of you. I can't see why you do it.*

I don't answer. I leave the house, I close the door without speaking and for some reason I don't cry, but the rest of the day tastes of my mother's words. The air tastes of her words. My food tastes of ashes. All day I keep from crying.

That same evening I come home from school. My mother serves dinner, and my father turns on the TV.

And then suddenly, right in the middle of dinner, I start to shout. I shout very fast and loud, closing my eyes, *Mommy gives money to Vincent, she's still doing it, I saw her give him some money the other day and she told me not*

*to tell you, she said whatever you do don't tell
your father, she wanted me to lie to you and—*
But my father doesn't let me finish the sentence. He interrupts before I can get to the
end. He turns to my mother and asks her
whether it's true. *Is this some kind of joke?*
He raises his voice. *What the fuck is he talking about?* He stands up, clenching his fists.
He looks around the room. He doesn't know
what to do, not yet. I was sure this was how
he'd react.

I look over at my mother. I'm too curious
not to. I want her to suffer for having humili-
ated me in the morning,

I want her to suffer,

and I know that starting a fight between my
brother and my father is the best way to make
her suffer. When my eyes meet hers, she says,
You really are a rotten little shit. She doesn't try
to lie. She looks ready to vomit with disgust. I
bow my head. I start to feel ashamed of what
I've just done, but for now the pleasure of re-

venge is uppermost in my mind (later, shame
will be all that's left).

My father explodes. He can't contain him-
self. Whenever we lie to him he goes crazy.
He throws his wine glass, breaking it on the
floor. He yells, *I call the shots in this house,
nobody fucking goes behind my back.* And he
shouts so loud that it frightens my mother. It
frightens even her—who any other time, any
other day of her life, will tell you that she'll
never be scared of a man, other things maybe
but never a man, she's not like other women.
She takes me in her arms and she hides my
sisters behind her. She wants to get him to
calm down, *Everything's going to be all right,
honey, I'll never do it again.* But he doesn't. I
knew he wouldn't. He keeps yelling and now
my mother loses her temper, too. *Are you out
of your fucking mind? I warn you, if you hurt
a single one of my kids with that broken glass,*

I'll cut your goddamn throat, I'll fucking destroy you. My father starts punching the wall, and he says, *What in God's name did I do to deserve a family like this, between that one over there—*

—he means me—

between that one over there, and this drunk over here who can't do a fucking thing except drink, and drink,

and drink,

just look at him,

he points his finger at my brother,

the loser. And it's then, when the word *loser* comes out, that my big brother stands and lunges for my father. He hits him to make him shut up. He slams my father's body against the wall, with all his mass, all his weight. Then cries of pain, insults, and cries of pain. My father doesn't do anything. He doesn't want to hit his son. He takes it. I felt my mother's warm tears falling on my head. I thought: *It serves her right, it serves her right.* She kept trying to hide my eyes, but I contemplated

the scene from between her fingers. I saw the
crimson blood stains on the yellow tiles.

I came close to being the one who would kill
you.

III.

PETER HANDKE SAYS: "No matter what happened my mother seemed to be there, openmouthed." You were not there. Your mouth wasn't even open, because you had lost the luxury of astonishment and horror, nothing was unexpected anymore because you no longer had any expectations, nothing was violent because violence wasn't what you called it, you called it life, you didn't call it, it was there, it was.

2004 or maybe 2005. I'm twelve or thirteen. I'm walking around the village with my best friend Amélie and we find a cell phone on the ground, on the asphalt. It was just lying there. Amélie was walking along and she tripped on it. The phone went skittering down the road. She bent down, picked it up, and we decided to keep it to play with, to send messages to the boys Amélie met online.

Within two days the police called to tell you I'd stolen a phone. I found the accusation overblown: we hadn't stolen anything, it was there on the street, by the side of the road, we didn't know who it belonged to. But you seemed to believe the police more than you believed me. You came to my room, you slapped me, you called me a thief, and you took me to the police station.

You were ashamed. You looked at me as if I had betrayed you.

You didn't say anything in the car, but once we were sitting before the policemen, in their office plastered with incomprehensible posters, you were quick to defend me, with a forcefulness I'd never heard in your voice or seen in your eyes.

You told them that I would never have stolen a phone. I had found it, that's all. You said that I was going to become a professor, or an important doctor, or a government minister, you didn't know what yet, but in any case that I was going to get a degree and I had nothing to do with delinquents [*sic*]. You said you were proud of me. You said you had never known a kid as smart as I was. I had no idea that you thought all those things (that you loved me?). Why had you never told me?

Several years later, once I'd fled the village and gone to live in Paris, when I went out at night and met men in bars and they'd ask how I got along with my family—it's an odd question, but they ask it—I would always tell them I hated my father. It wasn't true. I knew I loved you, but I felt a need to tell other people that I hated you. Why?

Is it normal to be ashamed of loving?

When you'd had too much to drink, you'd lower your eyes and say that no matter what you loved me, that you didn't know why you were so violent the rest of the time. You would cry, admitting that you couldn't make sense of the forces that came over you, that made you say things you'd instantly regret. You were as much a victim of the violence you inflicted as of the violence you endured.

You cried when the twin towers collapsed.

Before my mother you'd been with a woman named Sylvie. You had tattooed her name on your arm, yourself, in India ink. When I asked you about her, you wouldn't answer my questions. The other day a friend said, because

I'd been talking about you, *Your father doesn't want to go into his past because the past reminds him that he could have become a different person, and didn't.* Maybe he's right.

Those times I got in the car to ride along with you when you went to buy cigarettes, or something else, but usually and very often cigarettes, you'd put a pirated Céline Dion CD on the stereo—you'd written *Céline* on it in blue marker—you'd slip in the disc and you'd sing at the top of your lungs. You knew all the words by heart. I'd sing with you, and I know it's a cliché, but it's as if in those moments you could tell me things you could never tell me at any other time.

You used to rub your hands together before you ate.

When I bought sweets at the village bakery, you'd take one from the bag with a little guilty look, and you'd say: *Don't tell your mother!* All of a sudden you were the same age as me.

One day, you gave my favorite toy, a board game called Doctor Maboul, to the next-door neighbor. I played with it every day, it was my favorite game, and you'd given it away for no reason. I howled, I begged to have it back. You only smiled and said, *That's life*.

One night, in the village café, you said in front of everyone that you wished you'd had another son instead of me. For weeks I wanted to die.

2000 I remember the year because the Y2K decorations were still up around the house: crepe paper, colored lights, the scribbly drawings I'd brought home from school with gold letters spelling out good wishes for the new year and the dawn of the new millennium.

It was just you and me in the kitchen. I said, *Look Papa, I'm an alien!* and I made a face using my fingers and tongue. I never saw you laugh so hard. You couldn't stop laughing, you were gasping for air. Tears were running down your cheeks, which were bright, bright red. I'd stopped making my alien face but still you went on laughing. You laughed so hard that after a while I started to worry, frightened by this laughter that wouldn't stop, as if it wanted to go on for ever and echo to the end of the world. I asked why you were laughing so hard, and you answered, between two laughs, *You're the damnedest kid I've ever seen, I don't know how I could have made a kid like you.* So I decided to laugh with you. We laughed together, clutching our bellies, side by side, for a very, very long time.

The problems had started in the factory where you worked. I described it in my first novel, *The End of Eddy*: one afternoon we got a call from the factory informing us that something heavy had fallen on you. Your back was mangled, crushed. They told us it would be several years before you could walk again, before you could even walk.

The first weeks you stayed completely in bed, without moving. You'd lost the ability to speak. All you could do was scream. It was the pain. It woke you and made you scream in the night. Your body could no longer bear its own existence. Every movement, even the tiniest shift, woke up the ravaged muscles. You were aware of your body only in pain, through pain.

Then your speech returned. At first you could only ask for food or drink, then over time you began to use longer sentences, to express your desires, your cravings, your fits of anger. Your speech didn't replace your pain. Let's be clear. The pain never went away.

Boredom took up all the space in your life. Watching you, I came to see that boredom can be the hardest thing of all. Even in the concentration camps a person could get bored. It's strange to think about: Imre Kertesz says so, Charlotte Delbo says so, even in the camps, even with the hunger, the thirst, the death, an agony worse than death, the ovens, the gas chambers, the summary executions, the dogs always ready to tear a prisoner limb from limb, the cold, the heat, and the dust in the mouth, the tongue hardened to a scrap of cement in a mouth deprived of water, the desiccated brain contracting within its skull, the work, the never-ending work, the fleas, the lice, the scabies, the diarrhea, the never-ending thirst, despite all of it, and all the other things I didn't name, there was still room for boredom—the wait for an event that will never come or has been too long in coming.

You'd wake up early in the morning and turn on the TV while you lit your first cigarette. My room was next door. The odor of tobacco and the noise drifted in to me as the odor and noise of your being. The people you called your *buddies* would come drink pastis at our house in the late afternoon. You'd watch TV together. You'd go to see them from time to time, but more often, because of your back pain, because your back had been mangled by the factory, mangled by the life you were forced to live, by the life that wasn't yours, that wasn't yours because you never got to live a life of your own, because you lived on the outskirts of your life—because of all that you stayed at home, and usually they were the ones who came over. You couldn't get around anymore. It hurt too much to move.

In **March 2006**, the government of Jacques Chirac, then eleven years in office as president of France, and his health minister Xavier Bertrand, announced that dozens of medications would no longer be covered by the state, including many medications for digestive problems. Because you'd had to spend your days lying flat since your accident, and because you had bad nutrition, digestive problems were a constant for you. Buying medicine to relieve them became more and more difficult. Jacques Chirac and Xavier Bertrand destroyed your intestines.

Why do we never name these names in a biography?

In 2007, presidential candidate Nicolas Sarkozy leads a campaign against what he calls *les assistés*, those who, according to him, are stealing money from French society because they don't work. He declares: *The worker ... sees the* assisté *doing better than he is, making ends meet by doing nothing.* What he was telling you was that if you didn't work you didn't belong, you were a thief, you were a deadbeat, you were what Simone de Beauvoir would have called a useless mouth. He didn't know you. He had no right to think that: he didn't know you. This kind of humiliation by the ruling class broke your back all over again.

In 2009, the government of Nicolas Sarkozy and his accomplice Martin Hirsch replace the RMI—a basic unemployment benefit provided by the French state—with the RSA. You qualified for the RMI because you could no longer work. The shift from the RMI to the RSA was supposed to *incentivize a return to employment*, as the government put it. In truth, from that moment on, the state harassed you to go back to work, despite your disastrous unfitness, despite what the factory had done to you. If you didn't take the jobs they offered—or rather, forced on you—you would lose your right to welfare. The only jobs they offered you were part-time, exhausting, manual labor in the large town twenty-five miles from where we lived. Just getting there and back cost you three hundred euros a month in gas. Then, after a certain period, you were forced to take a job as a street sweeper in another town, making seven hundred euros a month, spending all day bent over gathering up other people's trash—bent over, even though your back was destroyed. Nicolas Sarkozy and Martin Hirsch were breaking your back.

You understood that, for you, politics was a question of life or death.

One day, in the fall, the back-to-school subsidy granted each year to the poorest families—for school supplies, notebooks, backpacks—was increased by nearly one hundred euros. You were overjoyed, you called out in the living room: "We're going to the beach!" and the six of us piled into our little car. (I was put into the trunk, like a hostage in a spy film, which was how I liked it.)

The whole day was a celebration.

Among those who have everything, I have never seen a family go to the seashore just to celebrate a political decision, because for them politics changes almost nothing. This is something I realized when I went to live in Paris, far away from you: the ruling class may complain about a left-wing government, they may complain about a right-wing government, but no government ever ruins their digestion, no government ever breaks their backs, no government ever inspires a trip to the beach. Politics never changes their lives, at least not much. What's strange, too, is that they're the ones who engage in politics, though it has almost no effect on their lives. For the ruling class, in general, politics is a *question of aesthetics*: a way of seeing themselves, of seeing the world, of constructing a personality. For us it was life or death.

In **August 2016**, during the presidency of François Hollande, the minister of labor Myriam El Khomri, with the support of the prime minister Manuel Valls, passed what was called the labor law. This law made it easier for businesses to fire an employee, and it allowed them to increase the work week by several hours beyond existing limits.

The company for which you swept streets could now ask you to sweep even longer hours, to spend more of every week bent over a broom. The current state of your health, the fact that you can hardly move or breathe, that you can't live without the assistance of a machine, are largely the result of a life of repetitive motions at the factory, then of bending over for eight hours a day, every day, to sweep the streets, to sweep up other people's trash. Hollande, Valls, and El Khomri asphyxiated you.

Why do we never name these names?

May 27, 2017 In a town in France, two union members—both in tee shirts—are complaining to president Emmanuel Macron in the middle of a crowded street. They are angry, that much is clear from how they talk. They also seem to be suffering. Emmanuel Macron dismisses them in a voice full of contempt: *You're not going to scare me with your tee shirts. The best way to afford a suit is to get a job.* Anyone who hasn't got the money to buy a suit he dismisses as worthless, useless, lazy. He shows you the line—the violent line—between those who wear suits and those who wear tee shirts, between the rulers and the ruled, between those who have money and those who don't, those who have everything and those who have nothing. This kind of humiliation by the ruling class brings you even lower than before.

September 2017 Emmanuel Macron condemns the "laziness" of those in France who, according to him, are blocking his reforms. You've always known that this word is reserved for people like you, people who can't work because they live too far from large towns, who can't find work because they were driven out of the educational system too soon, without a diploma, who can't work anymore because life in the factory has mangled their back. We don't use the word *lazy* to describe a boss who sits in an office all day ordering other people around. We'd never say that. When I was little, you were always saying, obsessively, *I'm not lazy*, because you knew this insult hung over you, like a specter you wished to exorcize.

There is no pride without shame: you were proud of not being lazy because you were ashamed to be one of those to whom that word could be applied. For you the word *lazy* is a threat, a humiliation. This kind of humiliation by the ruling class breaks your back again.

Maybe those who read or listen to these words won't recognize the names I have just mentioned. Maybe they'll already have forgotten them, or will never have heard of them, but that is precisely why I want to mention them here, because there are murderers who are never named for their murders. There are murderers who avoid disgrace thanks to their anonymity or to oblivion. I am afraid, because I know the world acts under cover of darkness and night. I refuse to let these names be forgotten. I want them to be known now and forever, everywhere, in Laos, in Siberia and in China, in Congo, in America, beyond every ocean, deep within every continent, across every border.

Is everything always forgotten in the end?

I want these names to become as indelible as those of Adolphe Thiers, of Shakespeare's Richard III, of Jack the Ripper.

I want to inscribe their names in history, as revenge.

August 2017 The government of Emmanuel Macron withdraws five euros per month from the most vulnerable people in France: it re-

85

duces—by five euros—the housing subsidies that allow France's poorest people to pay their monthly rent. The same day, or a day or two later, the government announces a tax cut for the wealthiest in France. It thinks the poor are too rich, and that the rich aren't rich enough. Macron's government explains that five euros per month is nothing. They have no idea. They pronounce these criminal sentences because they have no idea. Emmanuel Macron is taking the bread out of your mouth.

*

Macron, Hollande, Valls, El Khomri, Hirsch, Sarkozy, Bertrand, Chirac. The history of your suffering bears these names. Your life story is the history of one person after another beating you down. The history of your body is the history of these names, one after another, destroying you. The history of your body stands as an *accusation* against political history.

*

You've changed these past few years. You've become a different person. We've talked, a lot. We've explained ourselves. I've told you how I resented the person you were when I was a child—how I resented your hardness, your silence, the scenes that I've just described—and you've listened. And I have listened to you. You used to say the problem with France was the foreigners and the homosexuals, and now you criticize French racism. You ask me to tell you about the man I love. You buy the books I publish. You give them to people you know. You changed from one day to the next. A friend of mine says it's the children who mold their parents and not the other way around.

But because of what they've done to your

body, you will never have a chance to uncover the person you've become.

Last month, when I came to see you, you asked me just before I left, *Are you still involved in politics?* The word *still* was a reference to my first year in high school, when I belonged to a radical leftist party and we argued because you thought I'd get myself into trouble if I took part in illegal demonstrations. *Yes,* I told you, *more and more involved.* You let three or four seconds go by. Then you said, *You're right. You're right—what we need is a revolution.*